英訳付き
折り紙帖
Origami Booklet
Using Edo Chiyogami

監修／小林一夫
Editorial Supervisor
Kazuo Kobayashi

はじめに

折り紙の心　日本の心

　この本を手にとったあなたは、日本の二つの文化にふれることができます。年齢を問わずだれでも楽しめる「折り紙」と、日本の伝統文様が描かれた美しい「江戸千代紙」の世界です。

　いまからおよそ1400年も昔、シルクロードを経て日本に伝わった異国の文化。それは、日本の風俗習慣に溶け合い、四季折々の自然にみがかれ、独特の図案と色彩の織りなす文様の世界を開花させました。この本では、さまざまな文様を描いた江戸千代紙で、鶴や着物、クリスマスツリーなど素敵な折り紙をつくって楽しむことができます。

　日本人の心をうつした江戸千代紙と創造性ゆたかな折り紙。その二つの魅力を持った本書は、海外へのおみやげとしてもきっと喜ばれるでしょう。

国際おりがみ協会理事長　小林一夫

Introduction

The Spirit of Origami and the Japanese Mind

You can experience two aspects of Japanese culture through this book. One is origami, which everyone can enjoy regardless of age, and the other is the beautiful world of traditional patterned paper called *edo chiyogami*.

About 1,400 years ago, exotic cultures were brought to Japan on the Silk Road. These gradually blended with Japanese customs and were refined with aspects of nature from the four seasons, opening the door to a world of unique patterns and beautiful colors. With this book you can create fun origami models such as the paper crane, kimono and Christmas tree using the charmingly patterned *edo chiyogami* provided.

The spirit of the Japanese can be seen in these *edo chiyogami* patterns and creative paper models. I am sure this book, with these two attractive aspects, will make a great gift for friends overseas.

K·Kobayashi

Kazuo Kobayashi
The Chairman of the International Origami Association

Contents

折り紙の心 日本の心 The Spirit of Origami and the Japanese Mind —————— 2

千代紙と日本の文様 About Chiyogami and Traditional Japanese Patterns ————— 10

この本の使い方 Using This Book ————————————— 12

この本で使う記号の意味 The Symbols Used in This Book ————— 13

基本の折り方 Basic Folds ————————————————— 15

兜
Kabuto

道成寺 Dojoji

17

鶴
Tsuru

椿文 Tsubakimon

19

着物
Kimono

牡丹に蝶 Botan ni Cho

21

ネクタイ
Necktie

小花 Kobana

23

馬
Horse

源氏車 Genji-guruma

25

クリスマスツリー
Christmas Tree

五崩し Go-kuzushi

27

サンタクロース
Santa Claus

檜格子 Hinoki-goshi

29

おしゃべり鳥
Talking Crow

市松 Ichimatsu

31

兎
Rabbit

小桜 Kozakura

33

金魚
Goldfish

青海波 Seigaiha

35

白鳥
Swan

雪花 Sekka

37

海老
Shrimp

鮫小紋 Samekomon

39

ピラミッドボックス
Pyramid Box

蝶文 Chomon

41

紙風船
Paper Balloon

鹿の子 Kanoko

43

動くハートと箸袋
Beating Heart & Chopstick Bag

矢羽根 Yabane

45

跳ぶ蛙
Jumping Frog

柳に燕 Yanagi ni Tsubame

47

小箱
Small Box

上：花菱 Hanabishi　　下：鱗文 Urokomon

49　　　　51

ペンギン
Penguin

立涌 Tatewaku

53

小鳥
Little Bird

菊立涌 Kiku-tatewaku

55

笑う犬
Laughing Dog

籠目 Kagome

57

海亀
Turtle

亀甲菊 Kikkogiku

59

蝙蝠
Bat

縦縞 Tatejima

61

エンゼルフィッシュ
Angelfish

鳳凰に桐 Houo ni Kiri

63

折り方 How to Fold the Models

兜 Kabuto —— 65

鶴 Tsuru —— 66

着物 Kimono —— 68

ネクタイ Necktie —— 70

馬 Horse —— 71

クリスマスツリー Christmas Tree —— 72

サンタクロース Santa Claus —— 73

おしゃべり鳥 Talking Crow —— 74

兎 Rabbit —— 75

金魚 Goldfish —— 76

白鳥 Swan —— 77

海老 Shrimp —— 78

ピラミッドボックス Pyramid Box —— 80

紙風船 Paper Balloon —— 81

動くハート Beating Heart —— 82

箸袋 Chopstick Bag —— 83

跳ぶ蛙 Jumping Frog —— 84

小箱 Small Box —— 86

ペンギン Penguin —— 88

小鳥 Little Bird —— 89

笑う犬 Laughing Dog —— 90

海亀 Turtle —— 92

蝙蝠 Bat —— 94

エンゼルフィッシュ Angelfish —— 95

千代紙と日本の文様

　千代紙とは、和紙に草花や動物などのさまざまな図柄を色刷りしたものをいいます。

　松竹梅や鶴亀など、千代（末長く栄えること）を祝う図柄（めでた柄）が多かったことから「千代紙」と呼ばれるようになったといわれ、また一説には、千代田城（江戸城の別名）の大奥の女中たちがよく使ったことからついた名だともいわれています。

　そのルーツをたどっていくと、京都の公家たちが手紙や和歌を書く紙に装飾をほどこしたことにはじまります。やがて中国伝来の文様や鶴亀などの吉祥柄を描くようになり、江戸時代に入ると錦絵の技法（浮世絵に用いられた木版多色刷り技法）や江戸の町衆の生活とも結びついて多彩な図案がデザインされるようになりました。こうして庶民に親しまれる「江戸千代紙」が生まれ、現在でも折り紙のほか、小箱などの細工物や人形の衣装などに広く用いられています。

　江戸千代紙に描かれる図柄の多くは日本の伝統文様です。大きく分けると、植物文様、動物文様、幾何文様（単純化・象徴化された図形が連続しているもの）、天象地文様（天地の様子や自然現象を図案化したもの）、器物文様（生活の道具や身のまわりの品々を図案化したもの）に分類されます。

　これらの文様は日本人の生活や風習と密接なかかわりを持ち、幸運を引き寄せたり、魔よけとしての意味を持つものもあります。現代でも着物や浴衣地、手ぬぐい、焼き物の器の絵柄などに見られるほか、有名ブランドの衣料品のデザインに応用される例も少なくありません。

　身近な草花や生きものを図案化し、文様に移しかえた先人の観察眼と造形力──。本書で紹介できる文様はそのほんの一部ですが、美しい千代紙から立体の「折り紙」を折りだすことで、日本の伝統文様のすばらしさを新たな角度から見直すことができるでしょう。

About Chiyogami and Traditional Japanese Patterns

What is *chiyogami*? It is traditional Japanese paper that has been printed with a variety of colorful patterns, such as flower or animal patterns.

Some say *chiyogami* got its name from the many delightful patterns printed on it that celebrate *chiyo*, or eternal prosperity. Two examples are the pine, bamboo and plum pattern and the crane and turtle pattern. Others say it was named after Chiyoda Castle, also known as Edo Castle, where it was often used by the female servants employed in the inner chambers of the shogun and his wives.

Looking back on its roots, we find that *chiyogami* was invented when court nobles in Kyoto began to decorate the paper on which they wrote letters and Japanese tanka poems. It eventually came to have good luck patterns such as traditional Chinese designs and the crane and turtle pattern printed on it. In the Edo era, the technique of *nishiki-e* (a multicolored woodblock print technique used in ukiyo-e) was utilized to depict everyday scenes from the lives of townsfolk in Edo, and many new bright and colorful designs were produced. *Edo chiyogami*, which was popular among the common people, was created in this way. Today it is still widely used for origami, decorative boxes, doll clothing and more.

Many of the designs printed on *edo chiyogami* are traditional Japanese patterns. They are classified as botanical patterns, animal patterns, geometric patterns (continuous simplified or symbolic figures), celestial patterns (designs found in the universe and natural phenomena) and utensil patterns (designs of everyday tools and personal articles).

These patterns are not only related to Japanese life, manners and customs, but are also thought to bring good luck and act as talismans against evil. Nowadays, they are still seen on kimonos and *yukatas* (cotton summer kimonos), hand towels and ceramics, and on famous brand name clothing.

The powers of observation and modeling of our ancestors, who made designs from the flowers and animals about them, were superb. In this book we will introduce you to just a few of their many inventive designs. You will see these marvelous and traditional patterns from a new perspective as you begin to create three-dimensional origami models with beautiful *chiyogami* paper.

この本の使い方
Using This Book

この本の千代紙を使って、
24種類の折り紙作品がつくれます。
また、それぞれの紙の説明によって
日本の伝統文様について知ることができます。

You can make 24 origami models with
the *chiyogami* paper found in this book.
You will also learn about traditional
Japanese patterns from the explanations
that accompany each paper.

1 つくりたい作品を選びます。
Choose a model you would like to make.

2 ミシン線に合わせて紙をカットします。
ミシン線にいちど折り目をつけてからカットするときれいに切り取ることができます。
Cut the paper along the perforated line.
In order to cut the paper neatly, first make a crease along the perforated line.

3 折り方の載っているページを開きます。 例) see page 65
Open to the "How to Fold" page for your model. See page 65 for an example.

4 折り図を見ながら番号順に折っていきます。
完成した作品は、見本の写真と同じ位置に図柄（文様）が見えるとは限りません。
Look at the diagrams and fold in order.
On your completed models, the patterns will not necessarily appear
in the same position as in the sample photos.

5 できあがったら、好きな場所に飾ったり、友だちにプレゼントしましょう。
After you have finished, you can display your creation anywhere you please
or give it to a friend as a present.

6 折り方がわかったら、ほかの紙でも折ってみましょう。好きな色や柄、
いろいろな大きさの紙でつくってみると、さらに折り紙の楽しさが広がります。
Once you have got the idea, try making the model with a different kind of paper.
You can enjoy making these origami models again and again by using different
sized papers of your favorite colors and designs.

ぜひ折り紙を
楽しんでください
We hope you enjoy
making origami!

この本で使う記号の意味
The Symbols Used in This Book

線の種類や矢印など、この本で使う記号の説明をします。
折り図を見るときに必要になるので記号の意味を覚えましょう。

Here we will explain the symbols used in this book, including the different folding lines and arrow marks. These symbols will help you understand the diagrams, so please remember them.

谷折り　Valley fold (dashed line)

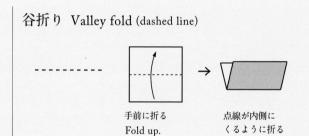

手前に折る
Fold up.

点線が内側に
くるように折る

折りすじをつける　Make a crease (fold and unfold)

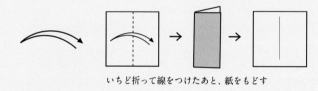

いちど折って線をつけたあと、紙をもどす

山折り　Mountain fold (dashed-dotted line)

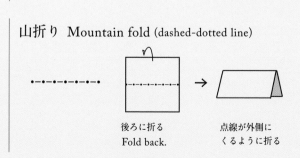

後ろに折る
Fold back.

点線が外側に
くるように折る

矢印の方向に折る　Fold in the direction of the arrows

The Symbols Used in This Book

紙の向きを変える Rotate

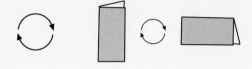

はさみを使う Use scissors

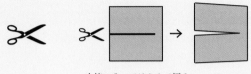

太線にそってはさみで切る
Cut along the thick line.

うらがえす Turn over

上下の位置は変えない
Do not change the orientation of the top and bottom.

紙のあいだを開く Insert fingers and open

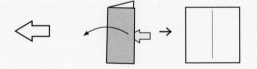

図を拡大する Enlargement

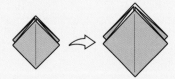

同じ幅・同じ角度 Same width, same angle

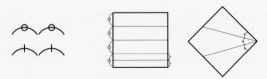

基本の折り方
Basic Folds

よく使う折り方です。とくに「四角折り」や「中わり折り」はよく使います。
These are the most common folds, especially the square base and the inside reverse fold.

四角折り Square base

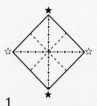 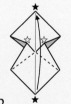

1
谷線、山線の折りすじ
をつける
Make valley and mountain
creases as shown.

2
★と★、☆と☆がつく
ようにたたむ
Fold to bring the matching
star points together.

3
できあがり
Finished!

三角折り Triangle base

1
谷線、山線の折りすじ
をつける
Make valley and mountain
creases as shown.

2
☆と☆がつくようにた
たむ
Fold to bring the star
points together.

3
できあがり
Finished!

中わり折り Inside reverse fold

1
折りすじをつける
Make a crease as
shown.

2
紙のさきを、内側に入
れるように折る
Push the point between
the layers and fold in.

3
できあがり
Finished!

かぶせ折り Outside reverse fold

1
折りすじをつける
Make a crease as
shown.

2
紙を上にかぶせるよう
に折る
Fold the paper over
as shown.

3
できあがり
Finished!

Basic Folds

段折り Pleat fold

1
山折りと谷折りをして、
段をつくる
Make one mountain fold and
one valley fold, like a pleat.

2
できあがり
Finished!

凧折り Kite base

1
半分に折って折りすじ
をつける
Fold in half (make a
valley crease).

2
開いて真ん中の線まで
折る
Open and then fold
both edges to the
centerline.

3
できあがり
Finished!

ざぶとん折り Blintz base

1
中心をつくる
Make a point at the
center.

2
4つのかどを中心に向
かって折る
Fold all 4 corners to the
center.

3
できあがり
Finished!

※中心のしるしのつけ方
How to make the center point:

軽く半分に折って、真ん中をおさ
えてもどす。別の向きから軽く半
分に折って、真ん中をおさえても
どす→×印がついたところが紙の
中心
Fold the paper in half lightly
and pinch the center, then
open. Repeat from the opposite
direction. The resulting cross
mark is the center point.

<ruby>兜<rt>かぶと</rt></ruby>

Kabuto : Samurai Helmet

兜は日本の侍のシンボルで、昔、
戦争のときにかぶったもの。現在
は男の子の成長と幸福を願って
「子供の日」に飾られます。

Kabuto are helmets that were
once worn in battle. They
have long been a symbol of
the samurai. These days they
are used as Children's Day
decorations to pray for the
growth and happiness of boys.

see page 65

道成寺
Dojoji

能楽「道成寺」や歌舞伎で着る衣装からきた丸紋尽くしの文様。丸紋には吉祥文（縁起のよい図柄）が描かれ、舞台では魔物を鎮める人物の衣装としてよく使われます。

This pattern of circles comes from costumes used in the Noh play *Dojoji* and in Kabuki performances. The designs in the circles bring good luck, so costumes with this pattern are often worn by characters that tame evil spirits.

鶴
Tsuru : Crane

これは日本の最も代表的な折り紙です。海外では『貞子の千羽鶴』のお話でも有名です。この鶴から基本的な折り方をたくさん学ぶことができます。

The paper crane is the most famous model in Japanese origami. It is well known from the story of *Sadako and the Thousand Paper Cranes*. Many basic folding patterns can be learned from this model.

see page 66

椿文
Tsubakimon

春の訪れを告げる椿は日本人に好まれ、着物にもよく描かれます。江戸時代には茶人らの影響で大変人気を呼びました。椿はCHANELのブランドモチーフとしても有名です。

The *tsubaki* (camellia) signifies the coming of spring in Japan. *Tsubaki* patterns are often found on kimonos. During the Edo era, tea ceremony masters made this into an extremely popular design. The camellia is also famous abroad as a Chanel brand motif.

着物
Kimono

まるで本物の日本の「着物」のように見える折り紙です。グリーティングカードに添えて使っても素敵です。

This looks just like a real Japanese kimono. It makes a wonderful decoration for greeting cards.

see page 68

牡丹に蝶

Botan ni Cho : Peony with Butterfly

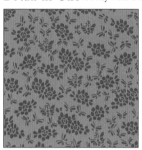

花と蝶を組み合わせた「花蝶文」のひ
とつ。牡丹は中国では百花の王とし
て「花王」と称され富貴の象徴でした。
高貴な香りは邪気を払い、蝶とともに
吉を呼ぶとされます。

One of many patterns that
combine flowers and butterflies.
The peony symbolizes wealth and
was called "the king of flowers"
by the Chinese. It is said that its
elegant scent chases away evil and
attracts good fortune along with
butterflies.

ネクタイ
Necktie

父の日のプレゼントに最適です。
この紙で3本つくれます。色や柄
を選んでみてください。

This origami necktie makes
an excellent Father's Day gift.
Three ties can be made with this
piece of paper. Choose a color
and design that your father will
like.

see page 70

小花

Kobana : Small Flowers

梅の花をモチーフにした愛らしい小花
文（梅花文）。気品があり香気の高い
梅は日本人にもっともなじみの深い花
で、平安時代には「花」といえば「梅」
をさしていました。

A charming pattern of small
flowers, in this case *ume* (Japanese
plum tree flowers). Many Japanese
adore the elegant and fragrant
ume blossom. When people said
"flower" during the Heian era,
they usually meant *ume*.

馬
Horse

これは中国伝承の折り紙からきて
います。この馬のシャープな姿は
みんなに人気があります。

This horse is a traditional
Chinese model. Everyone likes
his sharp looks.

see page 71

源氏車
Genji-guruma

公家が外出する際に使う牛車の車輪を
モチーフとした文様で「御所車」とも
いいます。平安時代の王朝文学『源氏
物語』の世界を象徴する文様です。

This pattern represents the wheels
of the ox-drawn carriages that
were once used by court nobles,
and is also known as the *gosho-
guruma* (carriage of the Imperial
Palace) pattern. It brings to mind
the Heian era world of court
literature such as *The Tale of Genji*.

クリスマスツリー
Christmas Tree

とても魅力的なクリスマスツリーです。最後に一回はさみを入れるだけで星ができて、みんなを驚かすことができます。

This is a very charming Christmas tree. Everyone will be amazed when you make the star on top of this tree with one simple snip of your scissors.

see page 72

五崩し
Go-kuzushi

和算や易（占い）で使う算木（計算用
の細長い板）を並べて図案化した文様
で「算木崩し」ともいいます。五本が
隣同士で互い違いに向きを変えている
ので「五崩し」です。

Sangi are long thin wooden blocks
that were once used in Japanese
mathematics and fortune-telling.
This pattern represents an
arrangement of groups of five (*go*)
sangi placed in alternating directions,
so it is called *go-kuzushi*. It is
sometimes also called *sangi-kuzushi*.

サンタクロース
Santa Claus

シンプルでとてもかわいいサンタ
です。クリスマスツリーやリース
につけたり、テーブルやプレゼン
トの飾りにも使えます。

This cute Santa Claus is easy
to make and can be used as an
ornament on your Christmas
tree or wreath. He also makes a
great decoration for the table or
presents.

see page 73

檜格子

Hinoki-goshi : Cypress Lattice

檜の薄板を斜めに組んだ垣根 (檜垣)
に似た幾何文様で、格子文に分類され
ます。「ヒノキ」の名はこの木を摺り
合わせて火を起こしたことに由来して
います。

One of many geometric patterns
that resemble traditional Japanese
lattice fences made of thin strips
of cypress. Because one can easily
start a fire by rubbing two sticks
of it together, cypress was given
the name *hinoki*, or fire tree, by the
Japanese.

おしゃべり烏
Talking Crow

つばさを動かすと、からすが話しているように見えます。これで子供たちと一緒に遊ぶと楽しいですよ。

He looks just like he is talking when you move his wings. It is fun to play with children using this crow.

see page 74

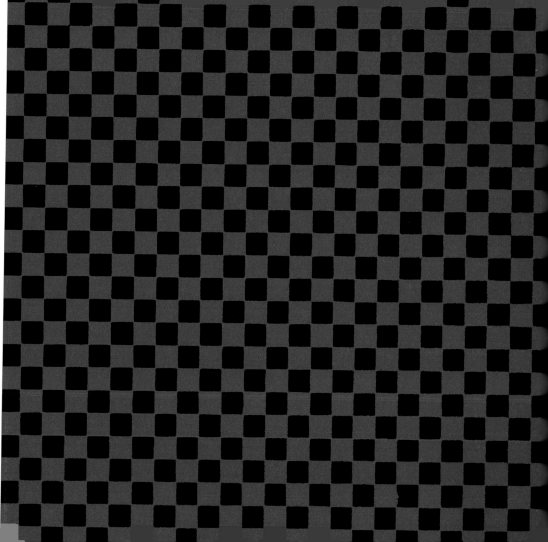

市松
Ichimatsu

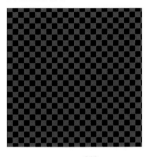

もとは「石畳」や「霰」と呼ばれていま
したが、江戸時代に中村座の人気役者・
佐野川市松が袴に用いたところ大流行
し、「市松文様」と呼ばれるようにな
りました。

This pattern was originally called
ishidatami (stone pavement) or
arare (hail). In the Edo era, it
became famous as the *Ichimatsu*
pattern when a popular kabuki
performer named Ichimatsu
Sanokawa used it for his *hakama* (a
long, pleated skirt-like garment).

うさぎ

兎
Rabbit

日本では秋に美しい月を見ながら
「お月見」としてお祝いする風習
があります。昔の日本人は月にう
さぎが住んでいると信じていまし
た。この折り紙は箸置きにも使え
ます。

In Japan, the beautiful harvest
moon is celebrated in a tradition
known as *o-tsukimi*. The ancient
Japanese believed that a rabbit
lived in the moon. This model
can also be used as a chopstick-
rest.

see page 75

小桜

Kozakura : Small Cherry Blossoms

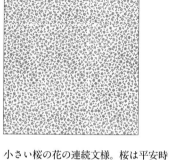

小さい桜の花の連続文様。桜は平安時代以降貴族に愛好され、梅に代わって「花」といえば「桜」をさすようになりました。文様として一般化したのは江戸時代からで、「小桜」の千代紙は昔から人気商品です。

This is a continuous pattern of small cherry blossoms or *kozakura*. After the Heian era, the cherry blossom was the favorite flower of the nobles. When they spoke of flowers, they now meant cherry blossoms rather than *ume*. This pattern has been popular since the Edo era, when *chiyogami* with the *kozakura* print was a best seller.

金魚
Goldfish

金魚は人気のある観賞魚です。兜
（17ページ）を折ったら、そこから
かわいい金魚に変身します。

The goldfish is a popular
aquarium fish. The *kabuto* (see
page 17) can be transformed
into this fish.

see page 76

青海波
Seigaiha

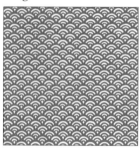

寄せ来る波をあらわす文様。海は生命
の源であり、同じ形が繰り返されるこ
とから、吉事が繰り返され一族が繁栄
するとされる吉祥柄です。

This pattern represents waves
lapping the seashore. Since the
sea is a source of life and its waves
neither change shape nor stop
repeating, it is a lucky pattern
that will bring good fortune and
prosperity to all the family many
times over.

海老
Shrimp

海老は日本人が大変好きな食べ物です。お祝いの席には欠かせず、お正月の飾りにも使われます。

Shrimp are a favorite of the Japanese. They are always served on festive occasions. This paper shrimp is often used as a decoration during the New Year's holidays.

see page 78

鮫小紋
Samekomon : Shark Skin

江戸小紋の代表的文様。細かな点を半
円状に重ねながら、微妙な変化を紡ぎ
だします。鮫の肌に似ていることから
こう呼ばれています。

This is a typical *edokomon* pattern
that was given its name because it
resembles shark skin. The many
overlapping semicircles of fine
spots convey a delicate feeling.

ピラミッドボックス
Pyramid Box

ピラミッド型のとてもおしゃれな
箱です。中になにか入れてプレゼ
ントボックスとして使えます。細
長いひもを2本とビーズを用意し
てください。

This is a very fancy pyramid-
shaped box. You can use it to
hold small presents. Please
prepare two long thin strings
and a bead for finishing.

see page 80

蝶文

Chomon : Butterflies

古来、蝶はその羽や舞う姿の美しさか
ら精霊の化身であると考えられ、さま
ざまな絵画や文様に描かれてきまし
た。この文様は蝶を巧みに図案化して
舞い集う様子を描いています。

Since butterflies have beautiful
wings and float gracefully through
the air, in old times they were
thought to be the incarnations
of human spirits and were often
depicted in pictures and patterns.
The pattern shown here cleverly
represents a gathering of dancing
butterflies.

紙風船
Paper Balloon

子供たちのための伝承折りのひとつです。手のひらでポンポンと弾ませて遊びます。いろいろな色や大きさの紙で折ってみましょう。

This balloon is traditionally made for children. You can play with it by bouncing it on your hand. Try making it with different colors and sizes of paper.

see page 81

鹿の子
Kanoko

細かな絞り染めの技法で生まれる文様。鹿の背中の白いまだら模様に似ているためこの名がつきました。日本の代表的な幾何文様で、少女の着物柄にも好まれます。文様がさらに細かく緻密なものは「匹田鹿の子」といいます。

This is a common Japanese geometrical design that is popular on girls' kimonos. It was originally created using delicate tie-dye techniques, and resembles the white spots on the back of a deer. An even finer spotted pattern is called *hitta kanoko*.

動くハートと箸袋
Beating Heart &
Chopstick Bag

このドキドキ動くハートは、老若
男女みんなのお気に入りです。バ
レンタインデーに「愛しています」
と告白するときにもおすすめ。動
くハートの残りの紙で箸袋がつく
れます。

This thumping heart is
everyone's favorite. It makes a
great Valentine's Day gift that
says "I love you!" You can make
the chopstick bag with the paper
left over from the beating heart.

see pages 82-83

矢羽根
Yabane

矢につける羽根の形を並べた文様で、
着物や工芸品などに幅広く用いられま
す。矢は本来武家のものですが「当た
る」ことから縁起がいいとして商家で
もよく使われました。

This pattern resembles the feathers
on the end of an arrow. It is widely
used in kimono designs and
crafts. Although only members
of the samurai class could possess
arrows, the *yabane* pattern was
often used by merchants' families
who thought it brought good luck
because arrows always hit their
mark.

跳ぶ蛙
Jumping Frog

指で背中を引くとピョンと跳ぶと
ても面白いカエルです。家族や友
だちと "カエル跳び" のレースを
楽しんでください。この紙で2匹
のカエルができます。

This jumping frog is so much
fun for everyone. When you
push his back down, he jumps.
You will have a blast jump
racing it with family and
friends. Two frogs can be made
with this paper.

see page 84

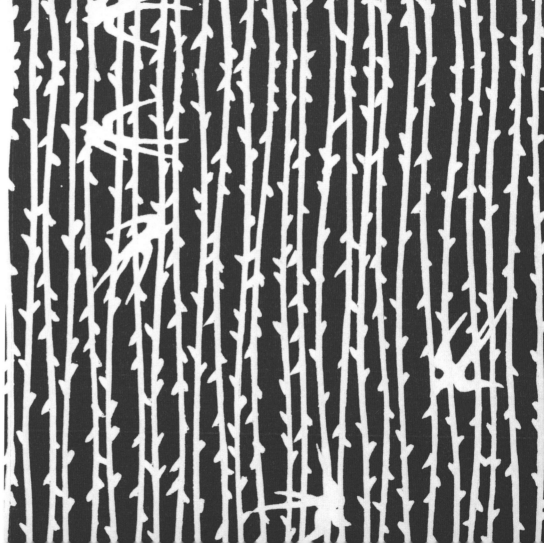

柳に燕

Yanagi ni Tsubame
: Swallows in the Willows

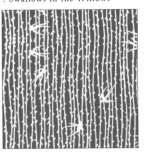

燕は春を告げる渡り鳥。水辺に植えられることの多い柳と組み合わせて、早春の情景を図案化した文様です。軽やかに飛ぶ燕が、枝垂柳とたわむれる様子が好まれました。

The swallow is a migrant bird that arrives in Japan in the spring. This pattern depicts an early spring scene of willows, which are often planted near the waterside, and swallows. People have always enjoyed watching swallows playfully flit among the branches of weeping willows.

小箱（上）
Small Box (Top)

シンプルな伝承折りの箱です。い
ろいろな色やサイズに折って、タ
ワーのように積み上げてみてくだ
さい。とてもきれいです。

This is a simple traditional
paper box. Try making many
boxes in different colors and
sizes. You can pile them up in a
beautiful tower.

see page 86

花菱

Hanabishi : Flower Chestnut

四弁の花を菱形に配した文様。古くは
身分の高い人たちだけが使うのを許さ
れていました。菱形は形が菱（沼や池
に群生する水草）の実に似ているため
こう呼ばれます。

A pattern in which four-petalled
flowers have been arranged to
make diamond shapes. In the past
only members of the upper class
could use this pattern. In Japan
the diamond shape is called *hishi*,
or water chestnut, because it looks
just like a water chestnut growing
in a marsh or pond.

小箱（下）
Small Box (Bottom)

この紙で箱の下の部分をつくります。折り方を覚えたら、いろいろな紙をつかって、ふたの部分との組み合わせを楽しんでください。

Use this paper to fold the bottom of your box. After you have learned how to make the box, try making the top and bottom in an assortment of color combinations.

see page 86

鱗文
Urokomon : Scales

三角形を連続させる文様で、魚や蛇の
鱗のイメージからこう呼ばれます。能
では鬼女の衣装となり、歌舞伎『娘道
成寺』では清姫が蛇身に変わる場面で
白地に銀の鱗文の衣装をつけます。

This is an unbroken pattern of
triangles that resembles the scales
of a fish or snake. In Noh plays,
female demons often have this
pattern on their costumes. In the
Kabuki play *Musume Dojoji*,
heroine Kiyo wears a silver-scaled
white kimono when she turns into
a snake.

ペンギン

Penguin

ペンギンは地上を歩いたり海の中
を泳ぐかわいいい鳥です。いろい
ろな大きさの紙で、ペンギン親子
をつくってみましょう。

The penguin is a cute bird that
walks about on the ground and
also swims in the sea. Try using
different sizes of paper to make
a penguin family.

see page 88

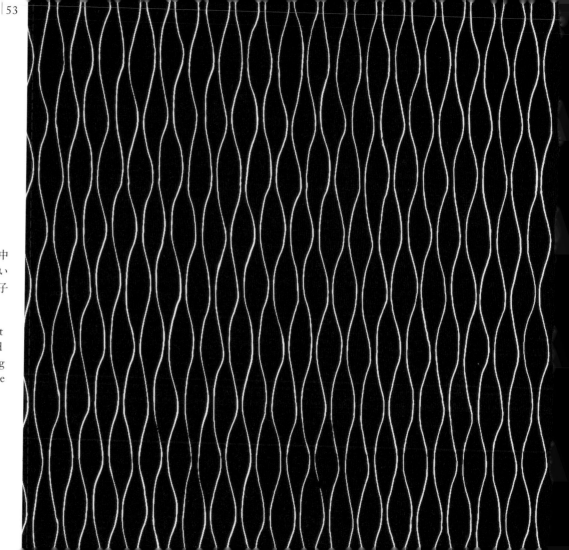

立涌
Tatewaku

「立涌」は水蒸気がゆらゆら立ち昇る様子を図案化したものといわれています。二本の曲線がふくらんだりしぼんだりする文様で、かつては身分の高い人たちだけが身につけました。「たちわき」ともいいます。

This pattern represents steam rising slowly through the air. As the two lines curve in and out the space between them narrows and widens. The *tatewaku* design used to be worn only by people of high position. It is sometimes called *tachiwaki*.

小鳥
Little Bird

伝承折り紙のひとつです。しっぽ
を長くして少し上にひっぱりま
しょう。バランスがよくなります。

This is a very traditional model.
If you make the bird's tail long
and pull it up a little, it will be
well-balanced.

see page 89

菊立涌
Kiku-tatewaku

「立涌」のふくらんだ部分に花などを
あしらうことで、さまざまなバリエー
ションがあります。菊は皇室の紋章で
もあり高貴なものを象徴します。花は
異なりますがヨーロッパのロゼット文
様（バラ花形）とよく似ています。

Many variations of the *tatewaku*
(steam) pattern have been created
by placing flowers in the wide
spaces between the wavy lines.
The *kiku* (chrysanthemum) is
the family crest of the Imperial
Household and symbolizes
nobility. Although the flower used
is different, this pattern is similar
to the European rosette pattern.

笑う犬
Laughing Dog

耳のたれた可愛い犬をつくりま
しょう。しっぽを持ってひくと頭
が動いて、笑っているようにも話
しているようにも見えます。

Try making this adorable dog
with big floppy ears. When you
pull his tail, he barks! He looks
as if he is laughing or talking.

see page 90

籠目
Kagome

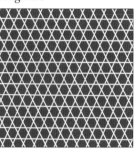

竹で編んだ籠の編み目を図案化した文
様。江戸時代、籠目は鬼が嫌うという
迷信があり、軒先に竹籠をさかさに吊
るして魔除けとする風習もありました。
竹と犬の組み合わせは漢字の「笑」に
似るため「招福」の吉祥文とされます。

This pattern looks like the weave
of a bamboo basket. In the Edo era,
people thought that ogres disliked
basket weave and often hung bamboo
baskets upside down from the eves of
their houses to ward off evil. When
the kanji character for bamboo (竹)
is placed on top of the character
for dog (犬), it looks almost exactly
like the character for laugh (笑). For
this reason bamboo and dogs are
considered to be a lucky combination.

海亀
Turtle

日本では、亀は長寿の象徴です。
縦横7.5cmの紙で可愛い子ガメ
が折れます。

In Japan, the turtle is a symbol
of longevity. You can make a
lovable baby turtle with a 7.5
cm square piece of paper.

see page 92

亀甲菊

Kikkogiku

亀は鶴と並んで長寿の象徴で、お祝い
の文様には欠かせないものです。これ
は亀の甲をあらわす代表的な吉祥文
で、平安時代には高位の官職だけが使
うことができました。

This is a common good luck
pattern of turtle shells. The turtle,
like the crane, symbolizes long
life. Turtle patterns are often used
on festive occasions. During the
Heian era, only high-ranking
officers could wear this design.

<ruby>蝙蝠<rt>こうもり</rt></ruby>

Bat

中国ではコウモリは福を呼ぶシン
ボルでもあるそうです。ハロウィ
ンの飾りに使えますね。顔を大き
めにつくるとかわいい感じになり
ます。

In China the bat is considered
to be a symbol of happiness.
This is a great decoration for
Halloween. If you make his face
large, he will look even cuter
than usual.

see page 94

縦縞

Tatejima : Stripes

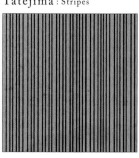

長い線が列をなす文様を縞柄と総称し、筋の位置で縦縞・横縞・格子縞に大別します。線の太い「棒縞」、線と線の間隔が不規則な「矢鱈縞」、縞目も見えないほど細かい「盲縞」など多数の種類があります。

Patterns made from long lines in rows are called *shimagara* (stripe) patterns. There are three main types of stripe patterns: vertical, horizontal and checked. Some common stripe patterns are the thick lined *bojima* pattern, the irregularly spaced *yatarajima* pattern, and the *mekurajima* pattern, the lines of which are so fine they can hardly be distinguished.

エンゼルフィッシュ
Angelfish

エンゼルフィッシュはおなじみの熱
帯魚です。この紙で2尾できます。
ラッピングペーパーや綺麗なプリ
ントの紙でも折ってみましょう。

Two of these common tropical
fish can be made with this
paper. Try creating colorful fish
using wrapping paper or other
bright print papers.

see page 95

鳳凰に桐
Houo ni Kiri

鳳凰は想像上の霊鳥で、中国ではすぐ
れた帝となる天子の誕生などの瑞兆
（よいこと、めでたいことの前兆）とし
てあらわれるといいます。桐は高貴な
木で、日本では菊とならんで皇室の紋
章となっています。

The *Houo* is an imaginary bird
that appears as a good omen when
a great emperor is born in Chinese
legend. *Kiri* (paulownias) are noble
trees, and are placed with the
chrysanthemum on the crest of the
Imperial Household.

兜 Kabuto [see page 17]

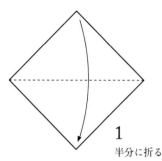

1

半分に折る

Fold in half.

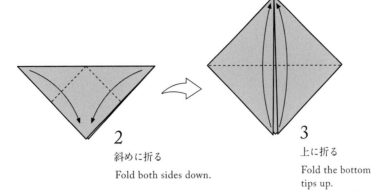

2

斜めに折る

Fold both sides down.

3

上に折る

Fold the bottom
tips up.

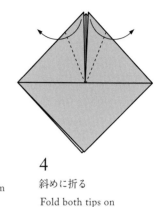

4

斜めに折る

Fold both tips on
the diagonal.

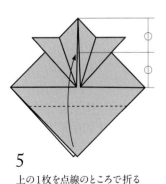

5

上の1枚を点線のところで折る

Fold the upper layer only along
the dotted line as shown.

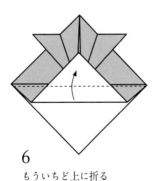

6

もういちど上に折る

Fold the bottom edge up again.

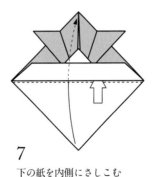

7

下の紙を内側にさしこむ

Fold the remaining triangle up
inside the helmet.

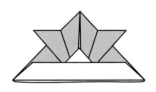

できあがり

Finished!

※このかたちから「金魚」
に変身します

You can change this model
into a goldfish (see page 76).

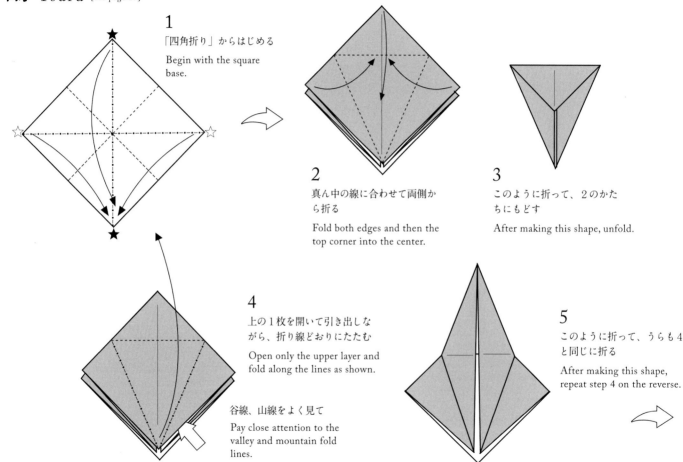

鶴 Tsuru [see page 19]

1

「四角折り」からはじめる

Begin with the square base.

2

真ん中の線に合わせて両側から折る

Fold both edges and then the top corner into the center.

3

このように折って、2のかたちにもどす

After making this shape, unfold.

4

上の1枚を開いて引き出しながら、折り線どおりにたたむ

Open only the upper layer and fold along the lines as shown.

谷線、山線をよく見て

Pay close attention to the valley and mountain fold lines.

5

このように折って、うらも4と同じに折る

After making this shape, repeat step 4 on the reverse.

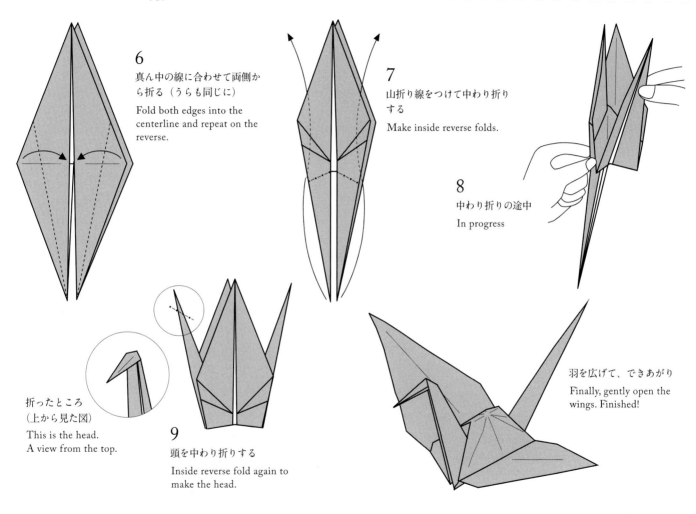

6

真ん中の線に合わせて両側から折る（うらも同じに）

Fold both edges into the centerline and repeat on the reverse.

7

山折り線をつけて中わり折りする

Make inside reverse folds.

8

中わり折りの途中

In progress

折ったところ（上から見た図）

This is the head. A view from the top.

9

頭を中わり折りする

Inside reverse fold again to make the head.

羽を広げて、できあがり

Finally, gently open the wings. Finished!

着物 Kimono [see page 21] ✂

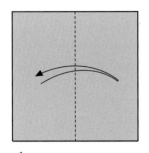

1

絵柄のある面を上にして、たてに半分に折りすじをつける

With the patterned side up, Fold in half and then unfold.

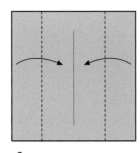

2

左右を中心に合わせて折る

Fold both edges to the centerline.

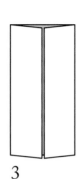

3

折ったところ

Make this shape.

うらがえす
Turn over

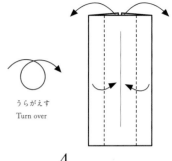

4

うら側の部分を引き出しながら、左右を中心に合わせて折る

Allowing the back sides to flip out, fold the edges to the centerline.

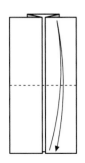

5

半分に折ってもどす

Fold in half and unfold.

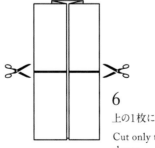

6

上の1枚に切り込みをいれる

Cut only the top flaps as shown.

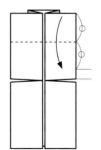

7

切り込みの少し上まで折り下げる

Fold the top down to a little above the cut.

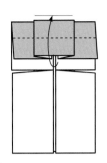

8

上端から少し上に出るよう
に折り上げる

Fold back again to a little
over the top edge.

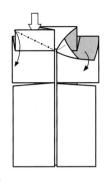

9

指を入れて上の1枚を開き
ながら折りたたむ

Insert a finger, open and
squash the collar.

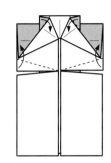

10

エリのかどと、袖下を少し
折る

Fold down both corners of
the collar and fold up both
corners of the sleeves.

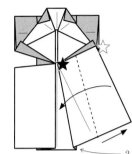

11-2

☆が真ん中の線に合うよ
うに折る（図12のかた
ちになるように）

Bring the ☆ marked
edge to the centerline
and fold. (it should look
like picture 12).

2、3ミリ残す
Leave 2 to 3 mm at
the bottom corner.

11-1

★をおさえ、下の部分を斜
めに引き出して折る

Hold at the ★ mark, then pull
the lower flap out diagonally.

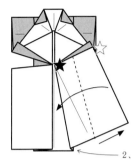

12

●が○に合うように斜めに
折る

Fold back diagonally,
ensuring that the ● and ○
marks match up.

左側も11-1,2、12を同様に
Repeat steps 11-1,2 and
12 on the left side.

2、3ミリ残す
Leave 2 to 3 mm at
the bottom corner.

13

図の位置で少し切り込みを
入れ、その下を谷折りする
（左側は折ったところ）

Make a small cut on each side
as indicated in the diagram and
valley fold the lower part (the
folded left side is shown).

うらがえして
Turn over

できあがり
Finished!

ネクタイ Necktie [see page 23]

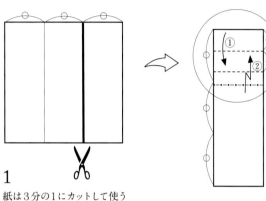

1

紙は3分の1にカットして使う
（カット線あり）

Use just 1/3 of the paper.

2

3分の1のところに山折りの
折りすじをつけて、①の谷折
りをする

Make a mountain fold 1/3 of
the way down the paper and
make valley fold ①.

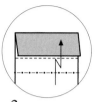

3

②の段折りをする

Make pleat fold ②
(from step 2).

4

このようにする

It should look
like this.

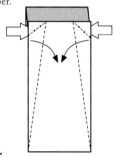

5

あいだを開いて、斜めに折る

Open the corners, squash, and
make the shape shown in step 6.

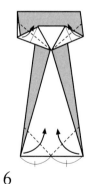

6

かどを4か所折る

Fold the four corners
shown up.

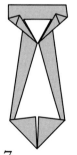

7

このようにする

Make this shape.

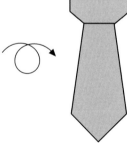

うらがえして、できあがり

Turn over. Finished!

馬 Horse [see page 25] ✂

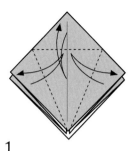

1

「四角折り」からはじめる（紙
が開いているほうを下に）。
点線で折って、もどす

Begin with the square base
(keeping the open side down).
Fold along the dotted lines and
unfold.

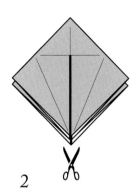

2

上と下の紙に切り込みを入れ
る

Cut along the center of both
the top and bottom flap.

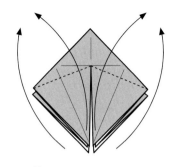

3

上の1枚を点線のところで折る

Fold the upper flaps along the
dotted lines.

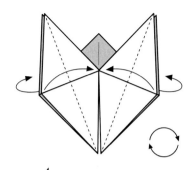

4

点線で谷折りする、うらも3
〜4のように折る

Make valley folds along the
dotted lines on both sides.
Repeat steps 3 and 4 on the
reverse side.

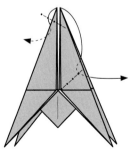

5

点線のところで、それぞれ中
わり折りする

Fold along the dotted lines and
make inside reverse folds to
make the head and tail.

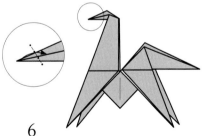

6

はな先を小さく折り込む

Fold in a tiny triangle to shape
the nose.

できあがり

Finished!

クリスマスツリー Christmas Tree [see page 27] ✂

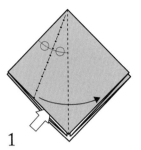

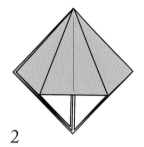

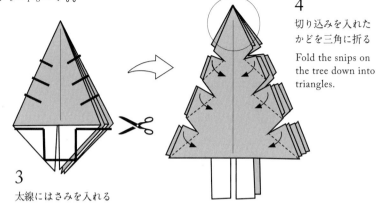

1

「四角折り」からはじめる。
4つあるひだに折りすじをつ
けて、開いて、つぶす

Begin with the square base.
Fold one flap in half to make
a crease. Then open and
squash it.

2

このようにする。残りの3つ
のひだも同じに

It should look like this. Repeat
step 1 on the remaining three
flaps.

3

太線にはさみを入れる

Cut along the thick lines.

4

切り込みを入れた
かどを三角に折る

Fold the snips on
the tree down into
triangles.

5

○のところに星をつくる。右
に5枚、左に3枚に分けて、
5枚のほうに切り込みを入れ
る（半分より少し長く、切り
落とさないように注意）

Make a star on top of the tree.
Divide the pleats so there are
five layers on the right and three
layers on the left. Cut a little
past the center line. Be careful
not to snip the top off.

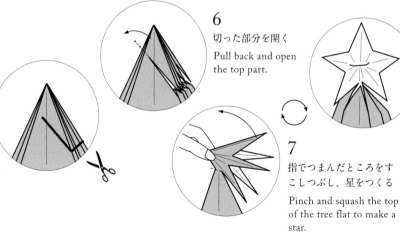

6

切った部分を開く

Pull back and open
the top part.

7

指でつまんだところをす
こしつぶし、星をつくる

Pinch and squash the top
of the tree flat to make a
star.

8

このようにする（開いたところ）

Make this shape.

できあがり
Finished!

サンタクロース Santa Claus [see page 29]

アレンジ／中島 進
Arranged by Susumu Nakajima

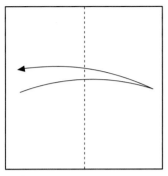

1

半分にして折りすじをつける

Fold in half and then unfold.

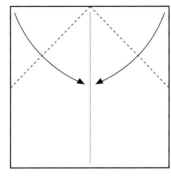

2

かどを真ん中の線に合わせて折る

Fold the corners to the centerline.

3

かどをもういちど、真ん中の線に合わせて折る

Fold the edges to the centerline.

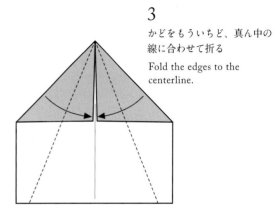

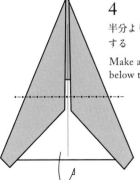

4

半分より少し下の線で山折りする

Make a mountain fold a little below the middle.

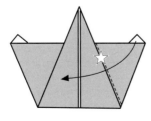

5

☆のところで前に折る

Fold inward along the star marked line.

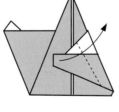

6

少しはみ出すように谷折りする。反対側も同じに

With a valley fold make an arm. Repeat on the opposite side.

うらがえして、できあがり

Turn over. Finished!

おしゃべり鳥 Talking Crow [see page 31]

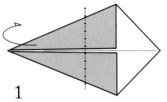

1

「凧折り」からはじめる
半分のところで山折りする

Begin with the kite base.
Make a mountain fold at the
halfway line.

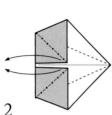

2

かどをつまんで、引くように
折る

Grab each corner and pull out,
folding as shown in step 3.

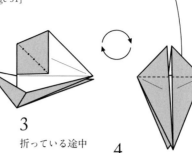

3

折っている途中

In progress

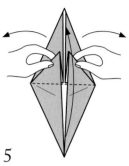

4

折りすじをつけて、うしろの
紙を上に折る

Make two valley folds as
shown. Lift the back flap up.

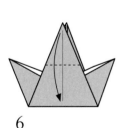

5

中の三角を外に引き出すよう
に折る

Pull the two triangles out as
you fold the front flap up. It
should look like step 6.

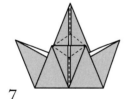

6

上の1枚を半分に折る

Fold the front flap
down and in half.

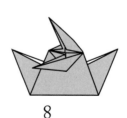

7

折りすじをつけてから、つま
むように折ってくちばしをつ
くる

Make the creases shown on
both the front and the back
flaps. Next open and pinch
along the lines as shown to
begin making the beak.

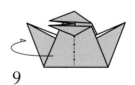

8

途中

In progress

9

半分に山折りして羽根をうし
ろで合わせる

With the 2 halves of the beak
as shown in 8, fold the body
back so that both wings come
together. The beak will form
naturally.

できあがり

Finished!

遊び方：羽根を両手で持って
開いたり閉じたりすると、く
ちばしがパクパク動きます。

How to play with the crow:
Hold his wings in both
hands. Open and close them
to make him talk.

兎 Rabbit [see page 33] ✂

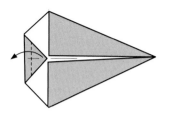

1

4等分した紙を使い、「凧折り」からはじめる（カット線あり）。少しとびだすように段折りする

Cut the paper into quarters and use one piece. Begin with the kite base as shown. Make a pleat fold in the top triangle, with the tip sticking out a little.

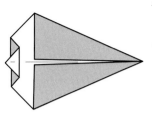

2

このようにする

It should look like this.

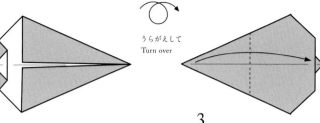

うらがえして

Turn over

3

半分ぐらいのところで折る

Fold in half as shown.

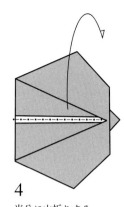

4

半分に山折りする

Fold in half along the centerline.

5

耳を上に引き上げる

Pull the ears up.

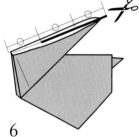

6

3分の2くらいまで切り込みを入れる

Cut about 2/3 of the way down the ears.

7

指で耳を広げてふっくらさせる

Open up the ears and shape them.

できあがり

Finished!

金魚 Goldfish [see page 35] ✂

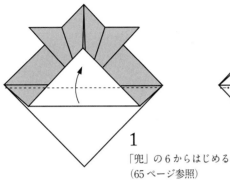

1

「兜」の6からはじめる
（65ページ参照）

Start from step 6 of the
kabuto (see page 65).

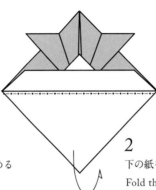

2

下の紙を山折りしてもどす

Fold the bottom triangle
back and unfold.

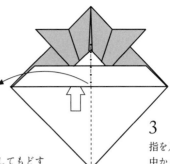

3

指を入れて中をひろげ、真ん
中から半分に折る

Insert fingers and open, then
fold along the lines.

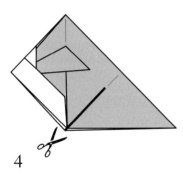

4

横にして切り込みを入れる
（うらも同じに）

Cut 2/3 of the top flap as shown
(repeat on the back).

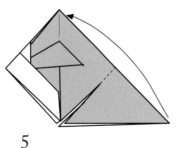

5

かぶせ折りする

Make an outside reverse fold.

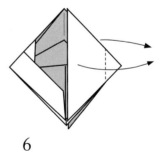

6

切り込みのところで谷折りし
て、かぶせ折りする

Make a valley fold where the
cuts end. Then make another
outside reverse fold as shown.

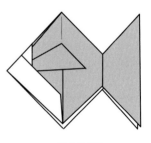

できあがり
Finished!

白鳥 Swan [see page 37]

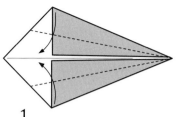

1

「凧折り」からはじめる
真ん中まで折る

Begin with the kite base.
Fold both edges to the centerline.

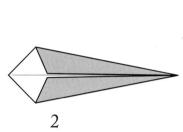

2

こう折れたら全部開く

Unfold this completely.

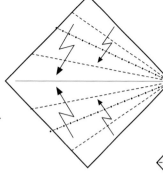

3

折り線をこのように変えて段
折りする

Change the creases as shown
and make pleat folds.

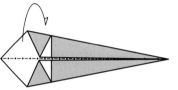

4

半分に山折りする

Fold in half along the
centerline.

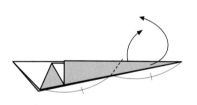

5

半分くらいのところからかぶ
せ折りで首をつくる

Make an outside reverse fold in
the middle to make the neck.

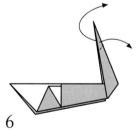

6

かぶせ折りで顔をつくる

Make an outside reverse fold
to forn the head.

7

くちばしを段折りする

Use a pleat fold to make
the beak.

羽根を広げてできあがり

Open its wings. Finished!

海老 Shrimp [see page 39] ✂

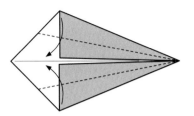

1

「凧折り」からはじめる
真ん中まで折る

Begin with the kite base.
Fold both edges to the
centerline.

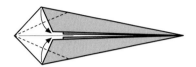

2

もういちど真ん中まで折る

Fold the top edges to the
centerline.

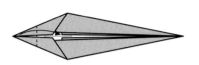

3

さきを谷折りする

Fold the tip forward.

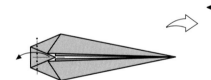

4

少し山折りしてもどす（段折
りをする）

Fold backward (make a pleat
fold).

5

4で折ったところを、はさみ
で半円形に切る

Cut a small semi-circle as
shown.

6

上の1枚にはさみで切り込み
を入れる

Cut only the upper layer into
two thin strips.

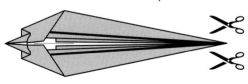

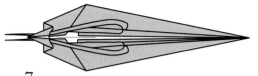

7

切った内側の2本を、穴に通す

Put the two thin strips through
the opening you made in step 5.

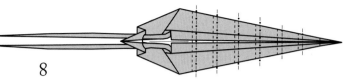

8

6か所くらい段折りする

Make six pleat folds down the
body.

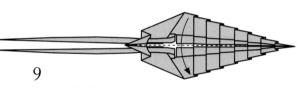

9

上下を半分に折る

Fold the whole body in half as
shown.

10

段を右下に引き出して、丸み
をつける

Pull each pleat down to make
the body rounded.

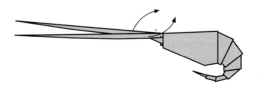

11

2本の触覚をうしろに折る

Fold the two thin strips back
like antennae.

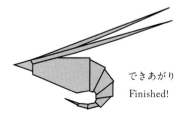

できあがり

Finished!

ピラミッドボックス Pyramid box [see page 41]

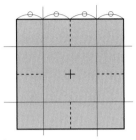

1

点線（谷折り線）の位置に折りすじをつける

With the patterned side up, make four valley creases as shown.

うらがえして
Turn over

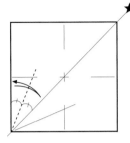

2

★の線に合うように、折りすじをつける（1でつけた折り線のあたりまで）

Make a short valley fold to the ★ marked line (make a half crease).

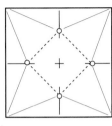

3

ほかのかども、すべて2と同じように折りすじをつける

Repeat step 2 on all corners.

4

1、2でつけた折りすじがまじわる点○をむすんで、谷折りで折りすじをつける

Fold four valley creases between the ○ mark points that were made in steps 1 and 2.

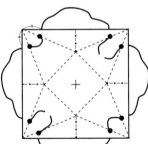

5

折り線を図のようにしっかりつける

Make the creases firm as shown.

●のところに穴をあけ、ヒモを2本通してひきあげ、ビーズを通す

Make holes at the ● marks and thread two strings through, then pull the strings up and close the top with a bead.

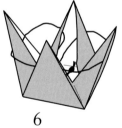

6

とじる途中

In progress

ビーズの上でひもをむすんで、できあがり

Make a knot above the bead. Finished!

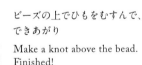

紙風船 Paper Balloon [see page 43]

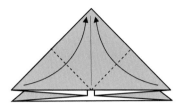

1

「三角折り」からはじめる
上のかどに合わせて折る

Begin with the triangle base.
Fold the bottom corners up to
the top.

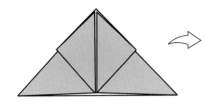

2

このようにする（うらも同じ
に）

Make this shape. Repeat on the
back side.

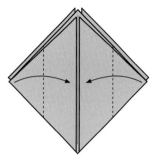

3

真ん中の線に合うようにかど
を折る

Fold both corners to the
centerline and repeat on the
back.

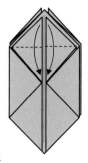

4

上の1枚を谷折りする

Fold the 2 top flaps down.

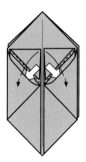

5

三角のポケットに4で折った
ところを入れる。4〜5をう
らも同じにする

Tuck the small triangles you
just made into the pockets and
repeat on the back.

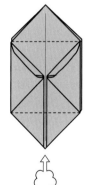

6

上と下に折りすじをつけて、
下のすき間からぷーっと息を
吹き込んでふくらませる

Make 2 creases as shown and
blow up the balloon.

できあがり
Finished!

動くハート Beating Heart [see page 45]

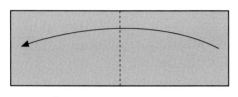

1

カット線で3分の1に切った
紙を横にして使う。
赤い色の面を表にして、半分
に折る

Use just 1/3 of the paper. With
the red side up, fold in half.

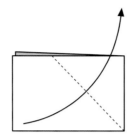

2

上の1枚を折る

Fold the top layer
up as shown.

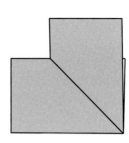

3

このようにする

It will look like this.

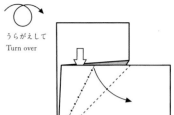

うらがえして
Turn over

4

折りすじをつけて、開いて、
つぶす

Make the crease shown,
open and squash.

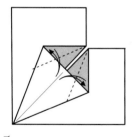

5

真ん中の線に合わせて、折り
すじをつける

Make creases by folding the
edges to the center line.

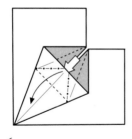

6

5でつけた折り線を使って、
開いて、つぶす

Open the diamond and squash
along the creases made in step 5.

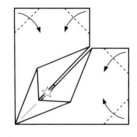

7

4つのかどを、少し三角に折る

Fold small triangles at the
corners shown.

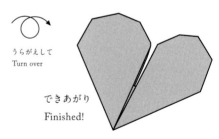

うらがえして
Turn over

できあがり
Finished!

遊び方：うらの☆のところをつまん
で引くと、ハートがドキドキ動きます。

To make the heart beat, pinch the
part marked with a ☆ and pull.

箸袋 Chopstick Bag [see page 45]

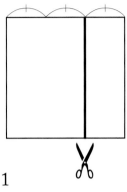

1

3分の2の幅の紙を使う（「動くハート」でカットした残り）。色の面を表にする

Use 2/3 of a piece of paper (the paper left over from the beating heart). Place the colored side up.

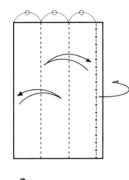

2

右端を少し山折りしてから、図のように谷折り線をつける

Fold the right side edge a little back and then make two valley lines as shown.

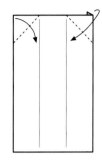

3

かどを2か所折る

Fold down the two corners shown.

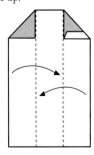

4

左側、右側の順で折る

Fold first the left, then the right side.

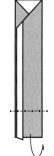

5

下を少しうら側に折る

Fold the bottom back.

できあがり

Finished!

跳ぶ蛙 Jumping Frog [see page 47]

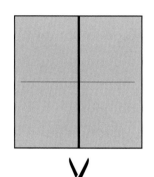

1
紙を半分に切る （文様のある面、色付きの面、好きなほうを表に使う）

Cut in half. You may place the side you like up (colored or patterned).

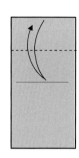

2
折りすじをつける

Make a crease as shown.

うらがえす
Turn over

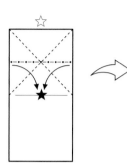

3
折りすじをつける

Make creases as shown.

4
三角折りのように折る （14ページ参照）

Make the triangle base (see page 14).

5
このようにする

It will look like this.

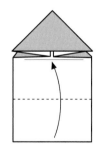

6
下を半分に折る

Fold the bottom in half.

7
両はしを真ん中に合わせるように折る

Fold the edges in so they meet in the center.

8
折っている途中 （三角はめくって、その下を折る）

In progress (lift the triangle a little and fold below it as shown).

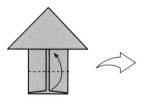

9
半分に折る

Fold the bottom in half.

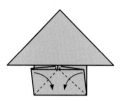

10

かどを三角に折る

Fold the corners down.

11

10 で折った紙を開いて、横に引き出す

Pull the triangles out from the tip to make a boat shape.

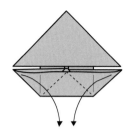

12

下に折る

Bring the flaps down as shown.

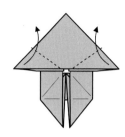

13

斜めにとび出すように折る（前足をつくる）

Fold the corners up diagonally to make the front legs.

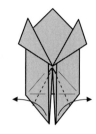

14

12 でつけた折り線に合わせて、折る（うしろ足をつくる）

Fold the two bottom flaps out along the lines at step 12 to make the hind legs.

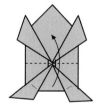

15

足のつけねのところで2つに折る

Fold in half at the point where all 4 legs meet.

16

半分折り返す

Fold down and in half again.

17

このようにする

It will look like this.

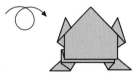

うらがえして、できあがり

Turn over. Finished!

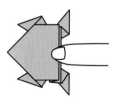

遊び方：背中を指でおさえてうしろにひくと、ピョンと跳びます。

How to make him jump: Just push his rear down.

小箱 Small Box [see pages 49 and 51]

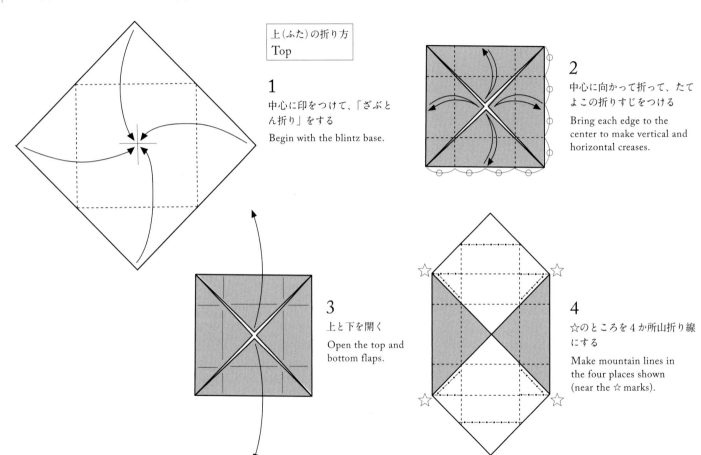

上（ふた）の折り方
Top

1
中心に印をつけて、「ざぶとん折り」をする

Begin with the blintz base.

2
中心に向かって折って、たてよこの折りすじをつける

Bring each edge to the center to make vertical and horizontal creases.

3
上と下を開く

Open the top and bottom flaps.

4
☆のところを4か所山折り線にする

Make mountain lines in the four places shown (near the ☆ marks).

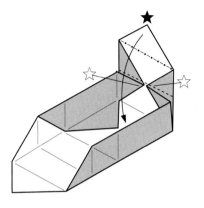

5

☆と☆をくっつけるように
折って、上の紙を内側へ折り
込む（★が中心につくように）

Bring the ☆ points together and
then fold the flap inside.

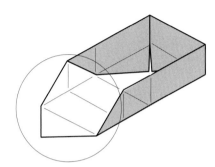

6

反対側も4、5を同様に

Repeat steps 4 and 5 on the
other sides.

できあがり
Finished!

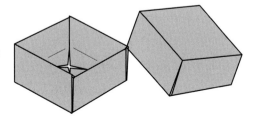

下（本体）の折り方
Bottom

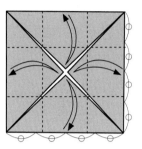

2-2

2で折りすじをつけるとき、
中心より1～2ミリ余分に折
る。そうすると上のふたより
一回り小さい箱ができ、ふた
が入りやすくなる。以下3～
6は同じ。

When making the creases in
step 2, bring each edge 1 or
2 mm over the center point
in order to make the bottom
a little smaller than the top.
Then follow steps 3 to 6.

ペンギン Penguin [see page 53]

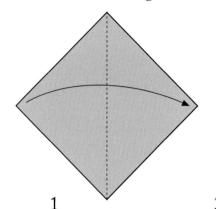

1

表を上にして半分に折る

With the patterned side up, fold in half.

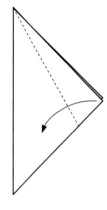

2

上の1枚を三角に折る（うらも同じに）

Fold the top layer to make a triangle (repeat on the back).

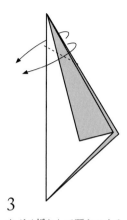

3

かぶせ折りして頭をつくる

Make the head with an outside reverse fold.

4

折り線をつけて中わり折りをして、おなかとしっぽをつくる

Make the tail with an inside reverse fold.

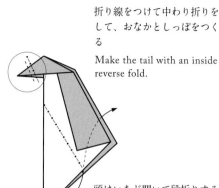

頭はいちど開いて段折りする（5、6参照）

Open the head to make a small pleat fold as shown in steps 5 and 6.

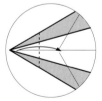

5

中に少し折る

Fold in a little.

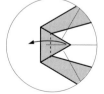

6

先がはみ出すように折る

Fold back (with the point sticking over the edge a little).

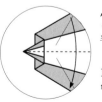

7

半分に折って、4のかたちにもどす

Fold in half and return to the shape of step 4.

できあがり

Finished!

小鳥 Little Bird [see page 55]

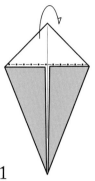

1

「凧折り」からはじめる
三角をうしろへ折る

Begin with the kite base.
Fold the triangle back.

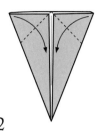

2

かどを真ん中の線に合わせて
折る

Fold the corners to the
centerline.

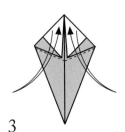

3

谷折りで折りすじをつけて、
2のかたちにもどす

Make valley lines and return
to the shape of step 2.

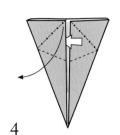

4

指を入れて開きながら、6の
かたちになるようにたたむ

Insert fingers to open and
fold down into the shape
shown in step 6.

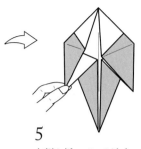

5

左側を折っている途中

In progress (left side)

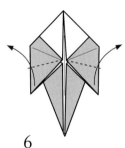

6

両はしを斜めに折る

Fold both tips up
diagonally.

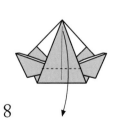

7

谷折りする

Make a valley
fold.

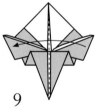

8

下に折って段折りをつくる

Fold down to make a pleat
fold.

9

全体を半分に折る

Fold in half.

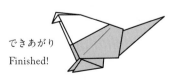

10

中わり折りして頭をつくり、
尾を斜めに引き上げる

Make the head with an inside reverse
fold, and pull the tail and up.

できあがり
Finished!

笑う犬 Laughing Dog [see page 57]

原案／ポール・ジャクソン
Originally by Paul Jackson

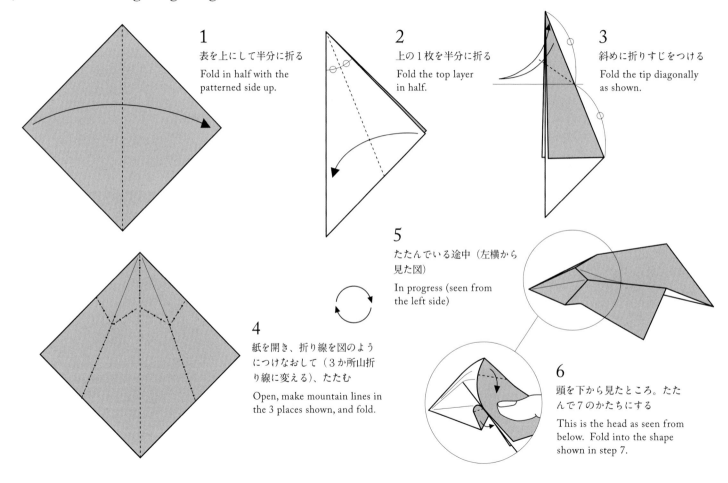

1

表を上にして半分に折る

Fold in half with the patterned side up.

2

上の1枚を半分に折る

Fold the top layer in half.

3

斜めに折りすじをつける

Fold the tip diagonally as shown.

4

紙を開き、折り線を図のようにつけなおして（3か所山折り線に変える）、たたむ

Open, make mountain lines in the 3 places shown, and fold.

5

たたんでいる途中（左横から見た図）

In progress (seen from the left side)

6

頭を下から見たところ。たたんで7のかたちにする

This is the head as seen from below. Fold into the shape shown in step 7.

7
頭のところを開く
Open the head.

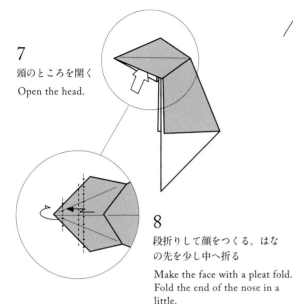

8
段折りして顔をつくる。はな
の先を少し中へ折る

Make the face with a pleat fold.
Fold the end of the nose in a
little.

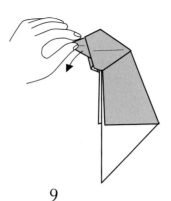

9
はなを少し下向きにする
Pull the nose down a little.

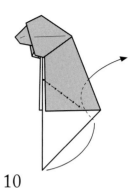

10
内側の紙を中わり折りして
しっぽをつくる

Make the tale with an inside
reverse fold.

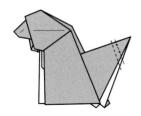

11
しっぽを開いて段折りする
Open the tale and make a
pleat fold.

できあがり
Finished!

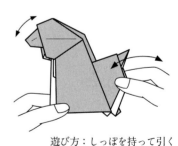

遊び方：しっぽを持って引く
と、顔を上下させます。
When you pull the dog's
tale, its face moves up and
down!

海亀 Turtle [see page 92] ✂

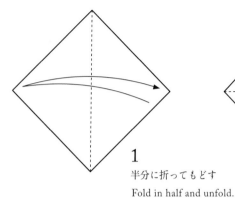

1
半分に折ってもどす
Fold in half and unfold.

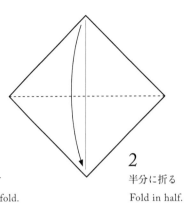

2
半分に折る
Fold in half.

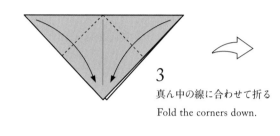

3
真ん中の線に合わせて折る
Fold the corners down.

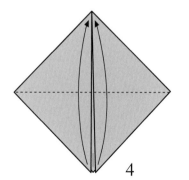

4
上の紙だけ半分に折る
Fold only the top flaps up and in half.

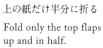

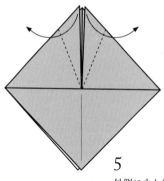

5
外側に少し折る
Fold out a little as shown.

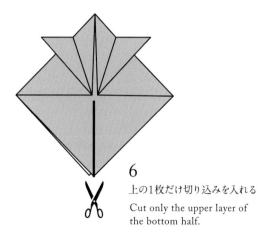

6
上の1枚だけ切り込みを入れる
Cut only the upper layer of the bottom half.

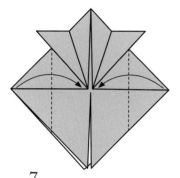

7

両はしを真ん中に向けて折る

Fold both corners in to the center.

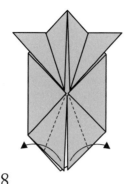

8

7で折ったところに合わせて、外側に折る

Fold the bottom flaps out as shown.

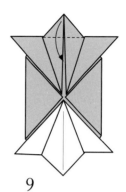

9

上のかどを折る

Fold the tip down.

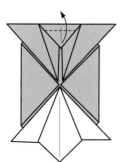

10

少しもどして、頭を出す

Fold back a little. This is the head.

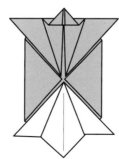

11

折ったところ

It will look like this.

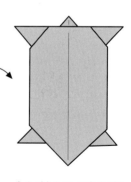

うらがえして、できあがり

Finished!

蝙蝠 Bat [see page 61] ✂

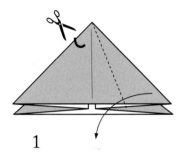

1

「三角折り」からはじめる。
2枚一緒に丸く切り込みを入
れて、右の1枚を真ん中の線
に合わせて折る

Begin with the triangle base.
Make a semicircular cut on the
left side. Next fold the top right
flap down to the centerline.

2

上の1枚を右にたおす

Fold the top left flap
over to the right.

うらがえす
Turn over

3

上の1枚を真ん中の線に合わ
せて折る

Fold the top left flap down
to the centerline.

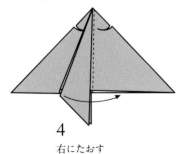

4

右にたおす

Fold to the right.

5

切り込みのところを前にたおす

Fold the top part down.

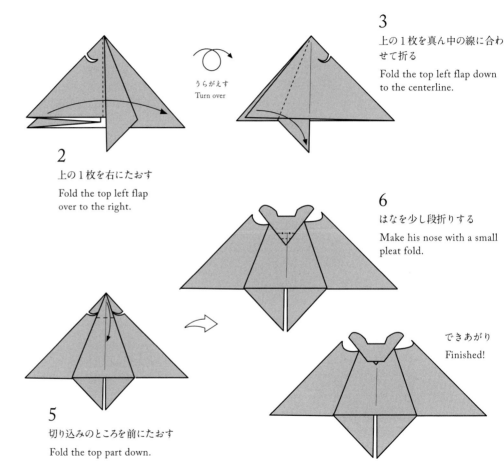

6

はなを少し段折りする

Make his nose with a small
pleat fold.

できあがり
Finished!

エンゼルフィッシュ Angelfish [see page 63] 原案／中島 進 Originally by Susumu Nakajima

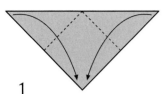

1

紙は対角線で斜めに切って使う（2匹つくれる）。
真中まで折る

Cut the paper in half along the diagonal. You can make 2 fish. Fold the corners down to the centerline.

2

外側まで折ってもどす

Fold both flaps back to the outer edges and unfold.

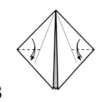

3

両はしに折りすじをつける（上の1枚のみ）

Make creases on both sides (upper layer only).

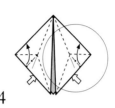

4

下から指を入れ、折り線を使ってたたむ

Insert fingers from the bottom and fold along the creases.

5

たたんでいるところ（拡大図）

In progress (enlargement)

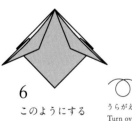

6

このようにする

It will look like this.

うらがえして
Turn over

7

点線で折ってもどす

Fold along the dotted lines and unfold.

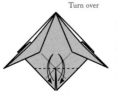

8

はさみで切り込みを入れる

Make a small cut.

うらがえして
Turn over

9

点線で折ってもどす

Fold the two bottom flaps up along the dotted lines and unfold.

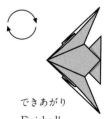

10

折り線を使って段折りする（尾びれをつくる）

Make skewed pleat folds using the creases to make the tail fin.

できあがり
Finished!

監修——小林一夫

1941年東京生まれ。内閣府認証NPO法人国際おりがみ協会理事長。お茶の水・おりがみ会館館長。全国の折り紙教室で指導や講演を行うかたわら、世界各国で折り紙や和紙を通じた国際交流、日本文化の紹介活動を行っている。著書多数。

Editorial Supervisor——**Kazuo Kobayashi**

Kazuo Kobayashi is the chairman of the International Origami Association (an incorporated nonprofit organization) and director of the Origami Center in Ochanomizu. He was born in Tokyo in 1941. He teaches and lectures origami classes all over Japan. He also organizes programs that use *washi* and origami to foster international exchange and introduce Japanese culture around the world. He has published many books about origami.

編集——宮下　真（オフィスM2）

アートディレクション——有山達也

デザイン——池田千草（アリヤマデザインストア）

撮影——石川美香

千代紙スタイリング——田中美和子

作品制作・折り図作成——湯浅信江

英文作成——吉田珠子

英文校閲——Sarah McNally

撮影協力——「ゆしまの小林」
　　　　　　お茶の水・おりがみ会館
　　　　　　URL http://www.origamikaikan.co.jp/

参考文献——『日本の文様』（小林一夫著・日本ヴォーグ社）
　　　　　　『文様の手帖』（小学館）
　　　　　　『日本の伝統デザイン』（学研）

英訳付き　折り紙帖

監修者　小林一夫

発行者　池田　豊

印刷所　図書印刷株式会社

製本所　図書印刷株式会社

発行所　株式会社池田書店
　　　　東京都新宿区弁天町43番地（〒162-0851）
　　　　☎ 03-3267-6821（代）／振替 00120-9-60072
　　　　落丁、乱丁はお取り替えいたします。

©K. K. Ikeda Shoten 2007, Printed in Japan
ISBN978-4-262-15245-5

0701903